Spectacular Sports

Flag Football

Subtraction

MW00803801

Dona Herweck Rice

Consultants

Colene Van Brunt
Math Coach
Hillsborough County Public Schools

Publishing Credits

Rachelle Cracchiolo, M.S.Ed., *Publisher*
Conni Medina, M.A.Ed., *Managing Editor*
Dona Herweck Rice, *Series Developer*
Emily R. Smith, M.A.Ed., *Series Developer*
Diana Kenney, M.A.Ed., NBCT, *Content Director*
June Kikuchi, *Content Director*
Susan Daddis, M.A.Ed., *Editor*
Karen Malaska, M.Ed., *Editor*
Kevin Panter, *Senior Graphic Designer*

Image Credits: pp.12–13 Derrick Neill/Dreamstime; p.18 Blulz60; all other images from iStock.

Library of Congress Cataloging-in-Publication Data

Names: Rice, Dona, author.
Title: Spectacular sports. Flag football / Dona Herweck Rice.
Other titles: Flag football
Description: Huntington Beach, CA : Teacher Created Materials, 2019. | Includes index. |
Identifiers: LCCN 2017054957 (print) | LCCN 2018006206 (ebook) | ISBN 9781480759763 (eBook) | ISBN 9781425856823 (pbk.)
Subjects: LCSH: Flag football--Juvenile literature. | Subtraction--Juvenile literature.
Classification: LCC GV952.2 (ebook) | LCC GV952.2 .R53 2019 (print) | DDC 796.332/8--dc23
LC record available at https://lccn.loc.gov/2017054957

Teacher Created Materials
5301 Oceanus Drive
Huntington Beach, CA 92649-1030
www.tcmpub.com

ISBN 978-1-4258-5682-3
© 2019 Teacher Created Materials, Inc.
Printed in China
Nordica.042018.CA21800320

Table of Contents

Fun for Everyone

People around the world play and watch sports. In the United States, some people like **football**. It is a fast game. Players pass, run, and kick.

Soccer is called *football* in many countries.

Football is a rough game!

Adults play
flag football.

There is another type of football. It is called flag football! It is a fun sport that almost anyone can play.

Kids play flag football.

Flag Football

Flag football uses most of the **skills** of football. Players in both sports must be quick. They must run and catch well.

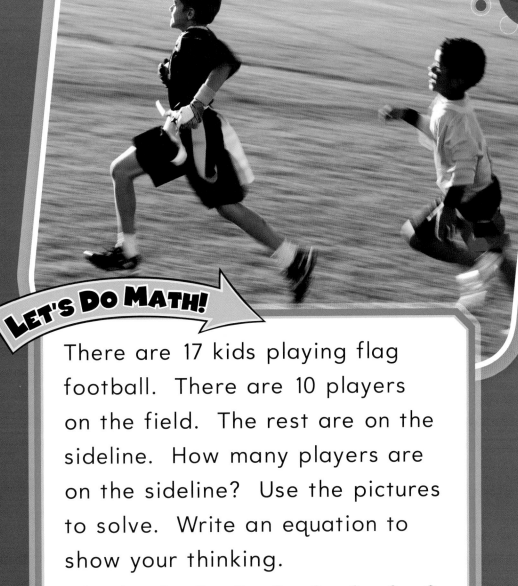

There are 17 kids playing flag football. There are 10 players on the field. The rest are on the sideline. How many players are on the sideline? Use the pictures to solve. Write an equation to show your thinking.

Players hold the ball and run. They pass the ball, too. But the two sports have one big **difference**. In flag football, there is no **tackling**. Instead of tackling, players pull flags.

Flags are long, bright strips of cloth. They are worn on players' belts or **tucked in** at the waist. The other team tries to pull off the flag of the player who is holding the ball.

There were 12 flags on the sideline. Some players took flags to wear during the game. Now there are 3 flags on the sideline. How many players took flags? Draw or place objects on a part-part-whole model to solve. Write an equation to show your thinking.

Whole
☐

Part	Part
☐	☐

How to Play

There are two teams in a game. The team with the ball tries to move it down the field. The other team tries to stop them.

A team scores a **touchdown** by running or catching the ball in the end zone. After a touchdown, a team gets the chance to earn another point.

LET'S DO MATH!

The Dolphins and the Sharks are playing a game. The Sharks score 9 points. The Dolphins score 14 points. How many more points do the Dolphins score?

1. Use the bar model to solve.

	?
Sharks	9	
Dolphins	14

2. Which equation can help you solve the problem?

A. $9 + 14 = \square$

B. $9 - 14 = \square$

C. $14 - 9 = \square$

What It Takes

Flag football takes skills! Players must be fast. They must use their feet, hands, and eyes to follow the ball and score. Most of all, they must want to have fun!

⚙️ Problem Solving

The big game is here! Answer the questions to track the teams' scores.

1. The Bears and the Lions each start the game with 0 points. Which symbol makes a true statement?

0_____0

A. >   **B.** <   **C.** =

2. At halftime, the Bears have 7 points. The Lions have 14 points. How many fewer points do the Bears have?

3. At the end of the game, the Lions have 3 fewer points than the Bears. The Bears have 20 points. How many points do the Lions have?

4. Who wins the game? How do you know?

Glossary

difference—the state of not being the same

football—a game in which two teams run and pass to score points

skills—things people can do from training and practice

tackling—forcing another person to the ground

touchdown—a score in U.S. or flag football worth six points

tucked in—folded or turned in

Index

Answer Key

Let's Do Math!

page 9:

7 players;
$17 - 10 = 7$

page 13:

9 players;
$12 - 9 = 3$

page 17:

1. 5 points

2. C

Problem Solving

1. C

2. 7 points

3. 17 points

4. Bears; 20 points is more than 17 points